better together*

*This book is best read together, grownup and kid.

 akidsco.com

a
kids
book
about

a kids book about

caring
for a pet

the
dodo

a
kids
book
about

A Kids Book About books are available online: *akidsco.com*

To share your stories, ask questions, or inquire about bulk
purchases (schools, libraries, and nonprofits), please use
the following email address: *hello@akidsco.com*

ISBN: 978-1-953955-88-3

Designed by Duke Stebbins and Gabby Nguyen
Edited by Emma Wolf

This book is for everyone out there who's in love with their pet (or will be soon!).

Intro

This book is all about what it means to take care of a pet. It's a big responsibility, but kids are totally up for it—especially because the fun is SO worth the hard work!

While kids will rely on their grownups for lots of things when it comes to caring for their pet, we make the case that the more kids get involved, the closer that special bond will be between them and their pet. We break down 12 things all pet owners need to do for their pets—from nourishing and keeping them clean, to socializing and playing with them, to empathizing with and loving them.

Kids can play an integral role in caring for their furry (or not-so-furry) friend, and the responsibility not only helps them grow, but builds the strongest friendship possible with their pet.

Taking care of
a pet is a really

responsibility.

Your pet needs your

help.

Pets rely on the human members of their family for some really important things they can't do for themselves.

We are here to share 12 important ways you can care for your pet. Let's dive in!

1. Nourish

Your pet needs nourishment,
just like you do.

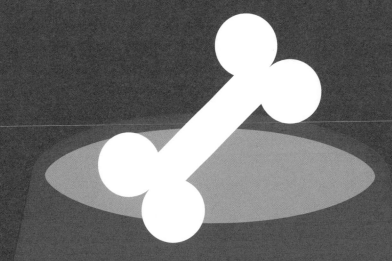

That means providing them with food that is just for them, not too much of it, and plenty of clean water in order to be strong, stay healthy, and be happy.

2. Clean

All pets get dirty.
And some pets like to
get REALLY dirty.

Cats can give themselves baths most of the time, but dogs...need your help.

They need to be bathed, but not as often as you do! Dogs produce natural oils, and too much bathing takes away the protection those oils provide for their skin.

3. Wellness

It's important to take your pet to a vet* for routine check-ups.

*Vet is short for *veterinarian*,
which is a doctor just for animals.

The vet will also check your pet's eyes, ears, nose, mouth, feet, tail, and bottom, as well as give them vaccinations.*

*A vaccine is a type of medicine, usually given through a shot, that helps protect the body from diseases and infections.

You can help them stay healthy by...

- talking to them in a comforting voice,

- creating a quiet space for them to get lots of rest,

- and making sure they are warm and dry when they get hurt or sick.

4. Protect

When a pet becomes part of your family, it's everyone's job to keep them safe.

Protecting your pet looks like keeping them out of dangerous situations and making sure they're OK both physically and mentally.*

Protecting your pet can also look like...

- being careful when meeting new people or animals,

- keeping your pet on a leash or in a fenced area,

- watching out for places that are too hot, too cold, or too noisy,

- or keeping dangerous things (like electrical cords) out of reach!

5. Communicate

Even though pets don't speak the same language we do, they "talk" to us a lot.

And with practice, you'll figure out what they're trying to say.

For example, if they wag
their tail, dance around,
or purr, they are probably happy
(or need to go outside!).

If they tuck their tail
or flatten their ears,
they might be feeling nervous.

You'll learn your pet's own special language by spending time with them, which is all part of **the bond you're building!**

6. Shelter

Just like people, pets need their own comfortable place to sleep (or just have some alone time).

Even if they love being outside, they need a warm and safe spot indoors where they feel secure.

When they are home alone, they'll likely go there too. You can help them learn how to feel comfortable!

7. Socialize

This one's BIG!

Socializing is helping your pet feel safe outside your family by spending time with other people and animals.

It can take awhile for pets to get used to new friends (humans AND animals), and you can help them feel safe by making sure everyone gives them plenty of time and space.

Eventually, your pet might develop some really strong relationships, and getting to see your pet hang out and play with their friends is magic.

We can't wait for that to happen for you!

8. Exercise

Pets

like

to

move.

It helps them maintain a healthy weight, get their energy out, and keeps their bodies working.

And if they're not moving as much as they should, you can help!

Learn how your pet likes to move!

Maybe they love playing chase or a special game you've made up like...hide the treat.

You can make an obstacle course for your cat out of cushions and boxes, or teach your dog to play fetch.

It can be a blast for both of you.

9. Teach

Have you ever heard the saying, "You can't teach an old dog new tricks"?

Yeah, that's not true.

Dogs (and all pets) love
to learn stuff. Especially when
there are treats involved!

Your pet needs YOUR help to learn important things, like walking well on a leash, how to sit and stay, and how to follow the rules to keep everyone safe.

And you can teach them
some fun stuff too, like
how to find food in a puzzle.

Your pet will love
picking up new skills because
you're the one teaching them.

10. Play

Lots of different things count as play for pets.

Exercise, new chew toys, balls of all kinds—they might even join you when you play make believe!

Your pet will want to do almost anything you are doing!

As long as your pet is using their body or brain and having fun, they're playing (and getting to know you better)!

11. Snuggle

Snuggling is DEFINITELY
one of the best parts
of taking care of a pet.

Cozying up on the couch
with your gigantic fluffy cat
or your little dog is soothing
for both of you.

And all pets need love,
even the ones who don't really
seem to want affection.

Learn where your pet's comfort zone is and keep them feeling supported the way they like best.

And if your pet isn't ready for lots of affection yet, just remember they will be comfortable one day and will show you love in a way that's just right.

It will be SO worth the wait.

12. Empathy

Your pet needs you to be the best friend you can be to them.

This means working to understand what they're thinking and feeling, which is called having empathy.

Empathy means focusing your attention on someone so you can understand their experience.

Think of how it feels when someone pays attention to you.

Like, *really* pays attention and listens well.

It matters, right?

It will matter to your pet too.

And guess what?

They are really good at empathizing with you too.

It's part of the special bond between animals and humans!

It really comes down to this:
pets need to feel loved.

The most important thing you can do for your pet is **love them as a family member.**

And we can't think of
anything better than that.

Outro

Our hope is that this book empowers kids to help take care of their pet and understand the importance of this special kind of bond. We don't want them to feel overwhelmed by the prospect of helping to care for their pet—we really want kids to understand how important and multifaceted pet care is and be excited to help out.

Taking care of a pet is about keeping them healthy, but also about keeping them happy. We hope this book inspires kids to get involved as much as they can, recognizing it's one of the best ways to be the best possible friend to their pet.